Cats

Words by Dean Morris

Raintree Childrens Books
Milwaukee • Toronto • Melbourne • London

Library of Congress Number: 77-8118

    4 5 6 7 8 9 0 08 81 80

Printed and bound in the United States of America.

Library of Congress Cataloging in Publication Data

Morris, Dean.
    Cats.

    (Read about)
    Includes index.
    SUMMARY: An introduction to wild and domestic cats,
their common behavior patterns, and their individual
traits.
    1.   Felidae — Juvenile literature.   2.   Cats — Juvenile
literature.   [1.   Cats.   2.   Felidae]   I.   Title.
QL737.C23M67   599'.74428   77-8118
ISBN 0-8393-0002-6 lib. bdg.

This book has been reviewed
for accuracy by

Dr. Carol Stein
Curator, Museum of Zoology
The Ohio State University

Cats

Cats are found all over the world. They live in forests. They live in jungles. They live in the mountains.

Many cats live in houses with people. They are kept as pets. This is a mother cat with her kittens. The mother takes care of the kittens. She feeds them. She washes their coats. Later she trains them to clean themselves. The kittens learn to hunt for their own food too. They learn to pounce and catch things with their claws.

Pet kittens are playful. So are baby lions and tigers. But they become fierce when they grow up.

Egyptian cat goddess

In long-ago times people thought that cats were gods.

People who lived in Egypt made statues of them. A statue of one Egyptian goddess was shown with a cat's head.

Freya and her cat

statue of sacred cat

People who lived in northern countries long ago believed in a goddess named Freya. Freya rode on a cat. We know about Freya from pictures and stories.

Many people believe cats have special powers. Some people think black cats bring bad luck. Some think they bring good luck. We often think of cats when we think of witches and magic.

Saber-toothed tigers were some of the first cats.

They lived at a time when ice covered much of the earth. The saber-toothed tigers died out thousands of years ago.

saber-toothed tiger

Saber-toothed tigers had large jaws and curved teeth. They were fierce and strong.

Early man hunted saber-toothed tigers. The hunters used spears and arrows to kill them. Then the men told stories about the tiger hunts. Maybe the stories made people think that cats had special powers.

All cats belong to the same family. Its name is the feline family. Felines have narrow bodies. They have strong muscles, especially in their hind legs. Their teeth are strong and sharp.

Cats have sharp, curved claws. They put them out when they are climbing or fighting. All cats, except the cheetah, can pull their claws in when they walk or rest.

paw

claw

strong
hind legs—

strong teeth

Cats wave their tails when they are playing or hunting food. The pet cat and the tiger both yawn and stretch in the same way.

Large, wild cats purr. They make a louder noise than pet cats. The big cat's roar is much louder than the pet cat's meow.

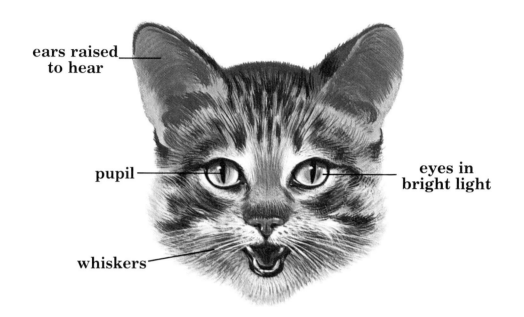

ears raised to hear

pupil

eyes in bright light

whiskers

Cats have good hearing and good eyesight. They can hear sounds from far away. When a cat hears a strange noise, it pricks its ears up. When a cat rests, its ears lie flat.

A cat's eyes have large pupils. The pupils get larger and smaller as the light changes. In bright light the pupils are thin slits. Cats do not see colors well.

However, cats can see very well in the dark. The pupils in their eyes open wide, and their eyes get more sensitive. Cats are able to hunt at night. They catch mice, birds, rats, and other small animals.

A cat's whiskers help it hunt. The cat uses its whiskers to feel its way in the dark.

Young kittens drink their mothers' milk.
Later, kittens learn to drink from a dish.
Pet cats need people to feed them and take
care of them. Cats that live with people
in their homes are called domestic.

Domestic cats still know how to hunt.
If they were lost or homeless, they would
hunt small animals for food.

domestic cat

Domestic cats come
from many faraway places.
Siamese cats were
once kept by kings and
queens. They used to
live in palaces in Siam.

Siamese

Manx

Other cats are also named for the place they came from. Manx cats came from the Isle of Man, near England. Burmese cats came from Burma. Persian cats came from Persia. There are mountains there. Persian cats have long, thick coats which protect them from mountain winds.

Many pet cats are tabbies. A tabby is a mixture of many different breeds of cats.

Burmese

Persian

wildcat

Some wildcats look very much like domestic cats, but the wildcats are larger.

Wildcats live out-of-doors. They hunt for their food.

Cats that live in the wild have to find their own food. They are good hunters.

This big cat is called a caracal. The caracal can run and climb very fast. It can stretch upward and kill a bird with one blow of its paw.

caracal

The lynx is a wild animal that lives in parts of North America and Europe. It is bigger than a domestic cat.

The lynx has a thick fur coat. Its tail is short and stubby. It has black tufts of hair on its ears.

lynx

The bobcat is a small lynx. It lives in parts of North America. Some bobcats live in forests. Others live in deserts.

Bobcats do most of their hunting at night. They hunt birds, mice, squirrels, rabbits, and other small animals. They are fierce and sometimes hunt animals larger than themselves.

bobcat

The tiger is one of the largest and most powerful wild cats. Tigers live in India and other parts of Asia.

Like many cats, the tiger has markings that make it hard to see. When the tiger is hiding in tall grass, its stripes look like shadows.

tiger

The lion is another very large wild cat. Most lions are found in Africa. A few are found in southern Asia.

A lion family is called a pride. The lion and the lioness both look after their babies. The young are called cubs. The parents train the cubs to hunt. This mother cleans and feeds her cubs just as domestic cats clean and feed their kittens.

cub

lioness

Some lions live in grasslands. Others live where there are sandy or rocky places.

Most hunt at dawn and dusk. Lions eat gazelles and other animals. Like all cats, lions sleep a lot.

male lion

**male lion
resting**

    Cats can rest and fall asleep almost
anywhere.

    This lion has found a good resting place
in the shade. If he falls, he won't
get hurt. Cats can twist their bodies
in the air and land safely on their feet.

black
leopard

Leopards are found
in Africa and Asia.
Most leopards have
light-colored fur with
black spots.

Some are all black.
Black leopards are
sometimes called
panthers.

leopard

When a cat hunts, it steps slowly and quietly. This way of moving is stalking. The cat creeps up on the animal it is hunting, called prey.

The leopard in the picture is stalking. Its spotted coat helps it hide in the tall grass. The leopard moves against the wind. The prey cannot smell the leopard coming.

leopard stalking

leopard climbing

Most cats are good at climbing. They use their claws to hold onto branches. Cats use their tails to help them keep their balance.

Leopards can climb trees very well. Their tails are especially long. Leopards' spots help keep them hidden as they climb trees.

The leopard cat is much smaller than the leopard. But the two animals are alike in many ways.

The markings on the leopard cat's coat are like the spots on a leopard.

The leopard cat is found in Asia. It often lives in the hills and hunts at night. It catches small animals for its food.

leopard cat

The jaguar is another cat that is like the leopard. Its home is in South and Central America, and it is the largest of the cats that live in America.

The jaguar often lives in thick forests. But it is not as good at climbing trees as the leopard.

Sometimes a jaguar's spots are so close together, the animal looks black.

jaguar

cub

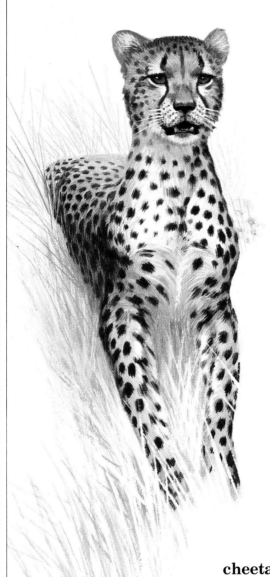

Cheetahs live on open plains in Africa. They usually hunt during the day. Cheetahs are among the fastest animals in the world.

When a cheetah sees its prey, it walks slowly toward it. Then the cheetah starts to run. It runs faster and faster.

As it reaches its prey, the cheetah throws itself at the animal. It brings the prey to the ground.

cheetah

The cheetah is sometimes called the hunting leopard.

This cheetah is chasing an antelope. The antelope can run very fast. If the chase does not last too long, the cheetah will catch the antelope. In a short race, cheetahs are able to outrun almost any other animal.

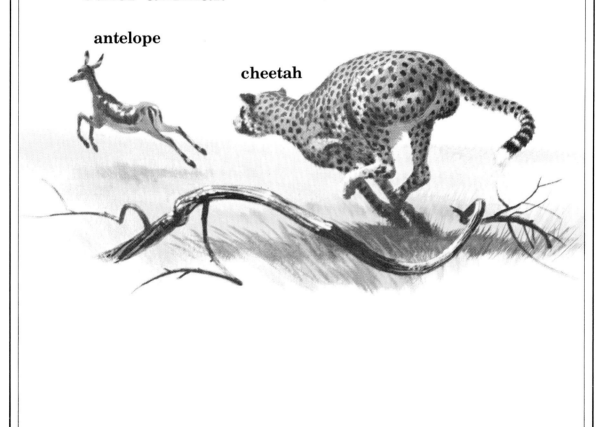

antelope

cheetah

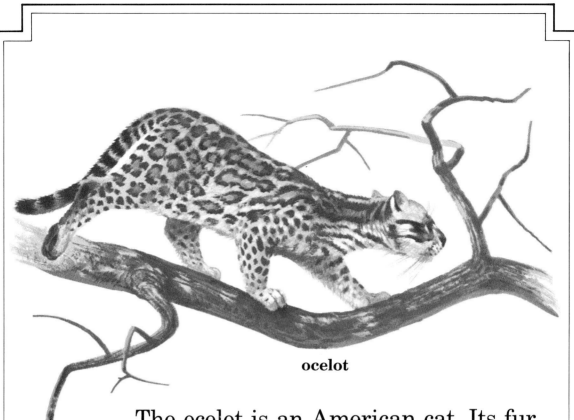

ocelot

The ocelot is an American cat. Its fur coat has both stripes and spots. The markings on its coat help the ocelot hide in the forest. The markings blend with the tree shadows.

Most cats do not like to be in water. The ocelot is different. It is a good swimmer. Sometimes it hunts fish to eat.

puma

The puma lives in rocky places of North and South America. This animal is sometimes called a cougar. It can leap from high places, land safely, and bound across the ground.

People used to hunt pumas because they killed cattle. Now laws protect the cats in many countries.

How Some Cats
Compare in Size

ocelot

lynx

cheetah

domestic cat

lion

puma

leopard

jaguar

bobcat

tiger

Where to Read About
the Cats

Pronunciation Key for Glossary

a	a as in **cat**, **bad**
ā	a as in **able**, ai as in **train**, ay as in **play**
ä	a as in **father**, **car**
e	e as in **bend**, **yet**
ē	e as in **me**, ee as in **feel**, ea as in **beat**, ie as in **piece**, y as in **heavy**
i	i as in **in**, **pig**
ī	i as in **ice**, **time**, ie as in **tie**, y as in **my**
o	o as in **top**
ō	o as in **old**, oa as in **goat**, ow as in **slow**, oe as in **toe**
ô	o as in **cloth**, au as in **caught**, aw as in **paw**, a as in **all**
oo	oo as in **good**, u as in **put**
o͞o	oo as in **tool**, ue as in **blue**
oi	oi as in **oil**, oy as in **toy**
ou	ou as in **out**, ow as in **plow**
u	u as in **up**, **gun**, o as in **other**
ur	ur as in **fur**, er as in **person**, ir as in **bird**, or as in **work**
yo͞o	u as in **use**, ew as in **few**
ə	a as in **again**, e as in **broken**, i as in **pencil**, o as in **attention**, u as in **surprise**
ch	ch as in **such**
ng	ng as in **sing**
sh	sh as in **shell**, **wish**
th	th as in **three**, **bath**
<u>th</u>	th as in **that**, **together**

GLOSSARY

These words are defined the way they are used in this book.

alike (ə līk′) the same way as; in the same way

antelope (ant′ əl ōp′) a thin, quick animal with long horns

anywhere (en′ ē hwer′) in any place

balance (bal′ əns) when all of the parts of something have the same weight, amount, or force as all parts of another

blend (blend) to mix together in a way that makes it hard to see the different parts of something

body (bod′ ē) the whole of a person, animal, or plant

bound (bound) to move by leaping, springing, or jumping

claw (klô) a sharp, curved nail on an animal's foot

curved (kurvd) to be bent in one direction

dawn (dôn) when light first appears in the morning; daybreak

desert (dez′ ərt) an area of hot, dry, sandy land with few or no plants

dish (dish) a plate used for holding food

domestic (də mes′ tik) to have to do with the home or family

dusk (dusk) the time of day just before the sun goes down

Egyptian (i jip′ shən) having to do with Egypt or its people

especially (es pesh′ ə lē) more than is usual

eyesight (ī′ sīt′) the ability to see

faraway (fär′ ə wā *or* fär ə wā′) at a great distance

feline (fē′ līn′) of or having to do with cats

god (god) someone or something believed to have special powers

goddess (god′ is) a female god

grassland (gras′ land′) land which has few or no trees and is covered with grass or grasslike plants

hidden (hid′ ən) to be kept or put out

of sight; not easily seen

homeless (hōm′ les) without a home

jungle (jung′ gəl) land in warm, damp places covered with many trees, vines, and bushes

law (lô) a rule made by a government for all people in a certain town, state, or country

meow (mē ou′) the sound made by a cat or kitten

mice (mīs) more than one mouse; see **mouse**

mixture (miks′ chər) something made up of two or more things put together

mouse (mous) a small animal with small ears, a pointed nose, and a long, thin tail

muscle (mus′ əl) body tissue in a person or animal made up of long, threadlike parts that tighten or relax to make the body move

northern (nôr′ <u>th</u>ərn) in or toward the north

onto (ôn′ to͞o *or* on′ to͞o) to a place on

outrun (out′ run′) to run faster than

palace (pal′ is) a very large, beautiful building where a king or a ruler lives

plain (plān) a large piece of land that is flat or nearly flat without any trees

playful (plā′ fəl) full of play

pounce (pouns) to suddenly leap on and take hold of something

power (pou′ ər) the ability to do or cause something out of the ordinary

powerful (pou′ ər fəl) full of power; having great power

prey (prā) an animal that is hunted by another animal for food

prick (prik) to be in a position of attention

purr (pur) the soft, low sound made by a cat

pupil (py o͞o′ pəl) the opening in the center of the colored part of the eye

rat (rat) an animal that looks like a mouse but is bigger

roar (rôr) the loud, deep sound made by some animals such as lions

sensitive (sen′ sə tiv) easily hurt or affected

shade (shād) a place where there is little or no sunlight

sharp (shärp) having a pointed end that can cut something easily

shown (shōn) to have brought to sight or view

slit (slit) a long, narrow cut or opening

spear (spēr) a throwing weapon with a sharp, pointed head attached to a long, thin handle

stalk (stôk) to follow prey slowly and quietly

statue (stach′ o͞o) a likeness of an animal or person made out of clay, stone, or some other material

stripe (strīp) a long, narrow band

stubby (stub′ ē) something that is short and thick

themselves (t͟hem selvz′ *or* t͟həm selvz′) the same ones

thousand (thou′ zənd) the number 1,000

tuft (tuft) a small bunch of hair, feathers, or other things growing together or fastened at one end and loose at the other

twist (twist) to wrap or turn around something

upward (up′ wərd) from a lower to a higher level or place

whisker (hwis′ kər) a long, stiff hair that grows near the mouth of some animals

wild (wīld) living or growing naturally without the care or help of man

witch (wich) a person who is thought to have magic powers

yawn (yôn) to open the mouth wide and take a deep breath

Bibliography

Arundel, Jocelyn. *Lions and Tigers.*
Edited by Russell Bourne and Natalie S. Rifkin.
Washington, D.C.: National Wildlife
Federation, 1974.

Bond, Gladys Baker. *Album of Cats.* Chicago:
Rand McNally & Company, 1971.
An introduction to the history, behavior, and
characteristics of twelve breeds of cats.

Burton, Maurice, and Burton, Robert, editors.
The International Wildlife Encyclopedia.
20 vols. Milwaukee: Purnell Reference Books, 1970.

Conklin, Gladys. *The Lion Family.* New York:
Holiday House, 1973.
Describes the family life and eating
and mating habits of Africa's fearless carnivore.

Johnson, Sylvia A. *The Lions of Africa.*
Minneapolis: Carolrhoda Books, 1976.

Pfloog, Jan. *The Tiger Book.* Racine, Wis.:
Western Publishing Company, 1976.

Wilson, Jean. *Animals of Warmer Lands.* Reading,
Mass.: Addison-Wesley Publishing Company, 1969.